MW00627541

the
little book
of
big knowing

TINY BURSTS OF INSIGHT
TO WAKE UP YOUR SOUL

michele sammons

For permission requests, write to the author, at: 1669 Peach Avenue, Memphis, Tennessee 38126.

The Little Book of Big Knowing/Michele Sammons —1st ed.

Hardback ISBN: 978-1-7361686-0-8
E book ISBN: 78-1-7361686-1-5

*Dedicated to
all the courageous Souls
who are taking the leap of faith
to remember.*

Contents

Dear Reader,

First of all, thank you!

Thank you for your time, your interest, and your willingness to stretch beyond your comfort zone by reading this little book.

I want to make a humble suggestion on how to get the most out of this book. I recommend you read it like it was written—in short bursts.

Let your intuition guide you. Maybe, start with one page a day. Perhaps, a few pages at a time. Read a little, put it down, and come back to the book again when you're ready.

You may find some insights that touch your heart so much you want to read them over and over. You may discover that some knowings stretch you a bit. It's all okay. Although you don't need it, you have my permission to take what resonates and chuck the rest; trusting, always, your own inner-wisdom above all else.

Thank you for joining me on this journey. I so appreciate you, and I am sending you big love.

Love,

Michele

Your Soul Has a Crush on You.

Your Soul is in love with you. You are the most beautiful, creative, intelligent, and fantastic creature it knows. You can do nothing to change its mind. Your Soul is going to love you until the end of time. It's an everlasting kind of love.

This Isn't a Solo Journey.

You can trust that you are not alone. You are loved, supported, tended to, guided, encouraged, focused upon, cheered, and held throughout your human experience.

You are surrounded by wise energy beings- teachers, guides, ancestors, healers, and masters. All of them are interested in your specific and personal well-being.

Celebrate Good Times! Come On!

Life is a celebration. Give yourself permission to have fun, laugh, smile, enjoy, dance, sing, skip, run naked, and make passionate love.

Celebrate the experience of living!

Coming Home.

You've embarked on an incredible journey. It's incredible because you're journeying home to your most intimate-self. Sometimes this self looks like creativity. At times, it can feel like spirituality; possibly the challenge of self-love or playful lightheartedness. It has many different flavors, but it all leads to the same place. Home. Home to self.

Choices.

What if there isn't one right choice of how to live your life? What if there is not a giant door with a sign on it that reads *The Right Choice— this way?* What if finding your purpose, career, or mate is more about making little decisions every day that feel good and naturally shift you into a place of Soul-alignment?

Here and Now.

Humans love to remember the past and dream about the future, but the only time that truly exists is the Here and Now. This beautiful present moment is where all possibilities live at once.

When you tap into the fullness of present moment awareness, you can access anything you want to know, be, do, or have. Everything is here waiting for you to recognize that it already exists.

You
are an
extraordinary
Soul.

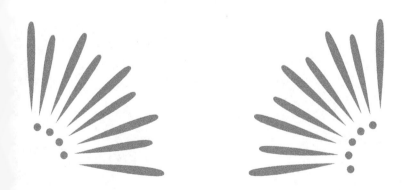

Desire.

Do you ever wonder where your desires originate? What makes you want to run a flower shop instead of a tire shop? These desires bubble up from within you. They emerge from the same place where your Soul dwells.

Spirituality Doesn't Have to Look Like Spirituality.

Your version of spirituality doesn't have to look like my version. You have the freedom to connect, commune, and enjoy your Soul in any way you choose.

This may look like meditation, yoga, baying at the moon, painting a mural, dancing in the street, banging on the drums, shooting hoops, cooking, walking in nature, and much more. The options are endless.

You'll know how you like to flow, express, and be in harmony with your Soul by the way it feels.

What You Put Out is What You Get Back.

It has been called many things—The Golden Rule, Karma, the Law of Attraction, and much more. At our core, we are energy beings. We create our realities from the inside out. What you feel on the inside, you will experience on the outside.

Most of us have not decided to be steadfast in what we want to feel, so the world looks like a jumble of good and bad experiences. When you choose to put how you feel above everything else, you'll experience a generous Cosmos delighting you at every turn.

What the Heck Does Allowing Mean?

Allowing, accepting, making peace with what is, surrender, and letting go are all the same energy. It's the vibration of letting the world be as it wants to be while you choose to recognize the perfection in the imperfect. Imagine that this allowing vibration can be achieved while witnessing anything—inner wounds, political chaos, unfairness, relationship drama, or even a loved one's death.

Intuition.

You are born with intuition. It's part of the human package. Why? Because as a Soul, you naturally sense, know, and communicate from this broader perspective. It's what you do.

Intuition is natural, and it's for everyone. Intuition, imagination, creativity are similar vibrations. When you are in that frequency, you are wise, alert, loving, and in-sync with life.

Ironically, the skill you have to learn as a human is to be analytical. Linear thinking is part of the human game. When you are in touch with your intuitive side you can bypass linear thinking to get answers fast—better known as quantum leaps!

You are
loved, supported,
and guided.

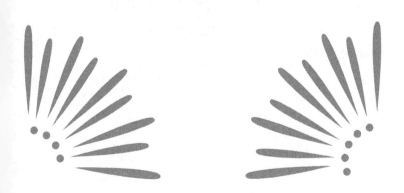

Should I Go or Should I Stay?

It's so easy to fall into the trap of wanting to make the perfect decision, but often this is a stalling tactic not to decide at all for fear of getting it wrong.

The split energy of indecisiveness feels uncomfortable because your energy is meant to flow.

The next time you must make a decision ask yourself, "What do I want?" And then permit that desire to be enough reason to go in that direction.

Take it for Granted.

Be grateful before something happens. Knowing that it will happen because you've asked.

Faith is believing before you see it. Appreciating the outcome before it happens because you know the Universe answered your request.

Timing.

It doesn't matter when you begin the process of remembering your original self. Any time of year, any age, any place in your life is the perfect place to start. It's never too late, or too hopeless, or too anything. Your Soul is waiting for you and rejoices when you begin. Wherever that is for you.

Sameness.

You exist because God wants you to exist. You are alive because you please Source. You please Source because you are Source. You are an extension of Source.

You are not just created in Its likeness. You are Its sameness.

Become Self-Conscious.

It's easy to live life on auto-pilot. Not really paying attention. Phoning it in.

But only by being fully conscious in the present moment of your thoughts, choices, desires, state of being, and actions can you genuinely know who you are.

Being self-conscious is being self-aware. Self-awareness is an inner listening of the Soul.

Listen intently, my friend. Listen consciously.

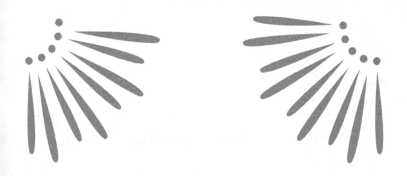

What you want
matters so much.

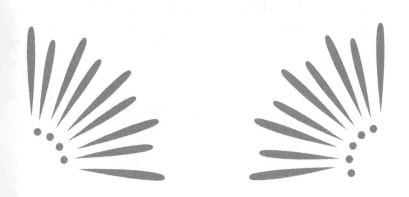

You've Got the Attention of God.

Imagine, if Source stopped thinking about you for one second, you would cease to exist. Because Source is paying attention to you, you are alive. He/She thinks about you constantly.

This constant thoughtfulness is interpreted by us as love. Whenever you feel the emotion of love you realize the presence of God. Just because you feel love only some of the time does not mean that God's love is not beaming to you all the time. It simply means you've stopped paying attention to God for a moment.

Redefine Everything.

Definitions give life meaning. Ever noticed that if you hear or read a new word, there is no emotional charge to it because you don't know what it means, but learn the meaning of the word, and you'll have some kind of reaction— positive or negative.

Enlightenment is about seeing everything without the preconceived definition, the judgment, or the projection. Your perception becomes fresh, new, alive in the moment.

A Friend in the Sky.

Every person on Earth has a personal counterpart in another dimension. A wise, ancient being that promised to guide you back home. This intelligent being is you. You are calling you.

While you're on Earth, you are continually receiving guidance from the Spirit-you. Some folks are more aware of the communication with this other dimension, but it's happening for everyone just the same. The messages are translated from your personal perspective, but all of us are receiving.

Divine Selfishness.

Selfishness is an act of honoring your Soul. It's listening to yourself, with your inner-ear, to what your heart wants. Divine Selfishness takes courage because you might disappoint the people you love when you listen to your heart. That's okay. Be willing to disappoint others to live your truth.

Calm Down Already.

The Cosmos is full to the brim with mystery. It's meant to be that way. What's the fun of knowing everything? It sucks the excitement out of discovery, wonder, creating anew, and awe. Relax. Enjoy the "ah-ha" moments and let the mystery reveal itself in delightful ways.

The Universe
has your back.

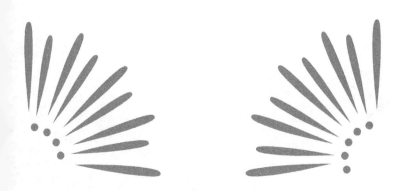

Value = Experience.

What you value is what you experience. If you want to call forth love, happiness, joy, peace, or enthusiasm, you must value it above all else. You have to make that your top priority. Everything else in your life becomes second to that core desire. Once you establish your core desire, the rest of your life begins to serve that purpose.

Bit by Bit.

When you come to a crossroads in your life, make the decision. Feel into whichever answer feels best in the moment and decide. Commit to that decision until there is another one to be made. One decision at a time. Little by little, until you turn around one day and can see the beauty of your path. The path you forged by listening to the call of your Soul.

Pushing Buttons.

Anything that pushes your buttons is asking for your love. Can you love your frustration, irritation, anger, and indifference? Can you love someone else's? Where can you apply the healing salve of love?

Do-Over.

You create your experience through your thoughts. If you don't like what you are experiencing, change your thoughts. Start over. Begin again. Your thoughts are like little magic wands, magically creating experiences for you.

Awareness of what you're thinking and deciding to think on purpose is mastery over perceived limitations. It takes a bit of discipline to become aware of thoughts and choose the ones you like repeatedly. But you can do it. You're thinking anyway. You might as well do it purposefully.

Paradox.

The facts, please. Just the facts. Humans love facts. We ask that you give it to us straight.

But the Universe is a giant Paradox. When we make peace with the paradoxical nature of Source, we can relax into the truth of the All that Is.

Enjoy
the ride!

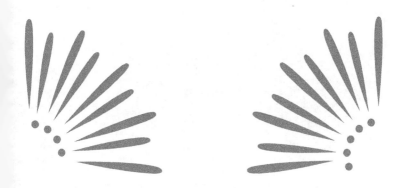

The Man in the Mirror.

As humans, we tend to identify with the image in the mirror. We look at that image and say this is me. This is who I am—this body, this face, this personality, this person. But you are so much more than flesh and bones.

As humans, our primary job, our main duty is to let ourselves experience the fullness of who we really are—the totality of our whole being by allowing spirit to flow through us in any given moment.

Bless Your Mess.

Find ways to appreciate your life, your job, your relationships, and your hardships. Hold your entire life in a loving gaze—finding the perfection in the imperfection. Celebrate everything!

Falling in love with your life is the way to find harmony with your total self.

The Next Step.

Sometimes desires arise just for the simple reason of being born, but usually, they form to get you to an experience, a junction with your Soul. Your Soul uses the pull of your most immediate, easy to receive desire to call you to something else.

The next step is never the final step. It always leads to another because you came here for the journey and the expansion of personal evolution.

God is Not Offended.

Don't worry. Your lack of attention to God doesn't offend him. He can't be offended. Nothing you do or say can hurt God's feelings. He/She is that mighty. That self-assured. That BIG. You can never offend God to the point He/She stops loving you.

How Free Do You Want to Be?

Freedom—true freedom—is loving everything and anything despite its appearances. This includes you. To be free, you must find a way to love yourself. Love yourself first, and allow that love to overflow into every thought, every decision, and every act.

You are a
magnificent
creator.

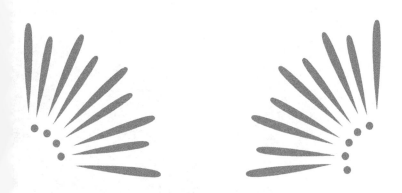

An Indulgent Universe.

God is always loving you. Loving you so much that Source never says no. You live in an indulgent Universe. Your desire is so important to God that He/She immediately says, "YES!"

Why would God say yes to everything you desire? Because you are Source, and God would never deny itself whatever it wanted. It is God. Its very nature is to create what It wants.

Stop Seeking and Start Finding.

Seeking is an integral part of the path for many spiritual folks. But, at some point, you must stop seeking in order to find. You must give up *the* hunt for the way to know *your* way. You must surrender the outer-quest for the inner-journey.

The kicker is that the inner-journey doesn't go anywhere. Your Salvation, Nirvana, Heaven, or answer was always inside of you. It's been there waiting for you to notice.

Compare and Despair—Oh My!

It's pointless to compare yourself to someone else.

Life is a giant Cosmic Ferris Wheel that you're on, and it is going round and round. Souls pop into human life for a new perspective. They want to view life through a new window. Maybe your wealthy boss is a Soul wanting to experience abundance in this lifetime, or perhaps that guy bumming on the corner is an Ascended Master wanting to exhibit God's beingness as humbly as possible.

This trying on new perspectives is part of the fun for the Soul. It likes to experiment with different viewpoints. So, it's not worth trying to figure out who is ahead or behind in the game of life. You've been at all points of the Cosmic Wheel, and you'll be at lots more points.

Relax. It's all good. It's all valuable.

Beaming.

Souls are beautiful things—effervescent, energetic, other-worldly. Amazing to think that a bright, light being would want to shrink itself down into a human body, but it does. As Souls, we find the human experience thrilling, challenging, and extremely Soul-satisfying.

You
are valuable
to the All-That-Is.

Creator.

Each life situation is another way to experience your capacity as a Soul. Never believe that you don't have the power to change your perspective. Or even change the energy within you. You are free to birth whatever you desire because, like your Soul, you are a creator—a creator at the core of your being.

Give Your Desire the Stamp of Approval.

Make your desires okay. Many times we try to talk ourselves out of our desires. They're too big, too selfish, take too long, not appropriate, not holy enough, not whatever.

Can you imagine that your desire is inspired by the inner you? Your desire is like a seed that is planted by your Soul. You don't/can't even fully understand why you have particular desires because they didn't originate with you.

Why You Can't Get it Wrong.

Life is not linear. From the broader perspective, there is no past and future. It's all Now. Everything is occurring right now.

Ponder this—every choice you make gets played out in the field of unlimited possibilities. And, every choice you didn't make gets played out too.

Why would your Soul want to play out all the options? Why not? Your Soul loves options and is not limited to only your human perspective.

In the broader picture, there are lots of versions of you out there living your life.

Souls Have Desires Too.

The Soul part of you knew for sure that the human experience would be worthwhile. You were so sure of it because your Soul's heart was telling you so.

Even as a Soul, we have desires that pull at us and call us. Desires so strong that we are willing to leave the non-physical realm and beam ourselves into a tiny baby body. The intertwining of spirit and form is a delicious act for our Soul.

It's All the Same Thing—God Stuff.

You. Me. Every bird. Tree in the forest. Concrete overpass. Shiny star in the night sky. It's all the same thing—God Stuff. There is only one Source of the magnificent Isness that everything is made of.

God forming into individualness and then reforming back into oneness, and reforming again into individualness is the cycle that goes on and on.

Imagine this process as God breathing in and out. Breathing into oneness and out again to individuals. So that God can experience being God from all perspectives. From the smallest perspective to the grandest perspective. All of it is God Stuff. All the time.

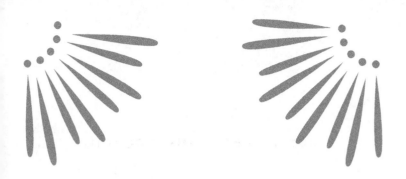

God is eternal energy
continuously
expanding
through you.

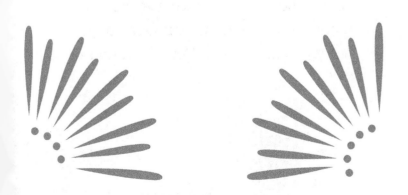

Don't Even Think About It.

You are constantly creating because that's what you are—a creator. You create your reality with every thought. It's important to deliberately choose what you think about. Select thoughts on purpose.

If you don't want something, literally don't give it a second thought.

If something is in your reality and you can't stop thinking about it, then accept it. Accept that it is there and then choose again. Say to yourself, "I see you. I accept you. Now, what do I want?"

Everything Changes.

Like it or not, everything changes. Bodies grow old, friends depart, jobs are lost, ecosystems die, music morphs, architecture evolves, and on and on. One of the keys to a happy life is to make peace with change. When you understand that the essence of you relishes this movement it makes it easier to accept. Your Soul thrives on the in-and-out of the experience. It's what keeps us all alive!

Mind-Blowing!

We like to think of our mind as existing in our brain, but really our mind is in our whole body. Every system, organ, cell, and atom contain consciousness.

Your beautiful mind-system is an extraordinary, sending-and-receiving, communication device. It's in constant contact with many realms— transmitting to the outer limits of the Universe.

You're not a Doing. You're a Being.

Somehow we've got it backward. We like to explain who we are by what we do. You'll often hear someone say, I'm an artist, writer, drummer, businessman, teacher, pilot, or farmer. But that's not who you are. That's how you express who you are.

You are a Soul who is creating life in the medium of artist, writer, drummer, etc.

You are a state of being—a vibration, a frequency, who creates through every thought, belief, action, and deed stemming from that state of being.

To create a joyful life, the key is to infuse your doing with your highest state of being.

Your Current Address is Heaven.

What if you already live in Heaven? Or better said, what if Heaven has the potential to live in you?

Heaven is not a place. It's a vibration. It's a state of being. You find Heaven when you dwell in the present moment without resistance. It is a frequency of knowing that all is well. Nothing needs to be perfected, changed, or improved.

Heaven is a choice. A moment to moment choice of living in the vibration of bliss.

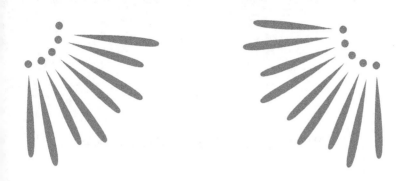

Dream Big.

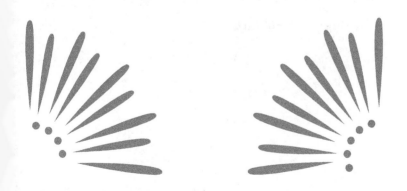

What's Got Your Attention?

Drama and trauma, big or small, can make you feel immersed in the human game. The drama's energy is so attractive that you become an active piece in the game instead of sitting in the center of yourself; seeing life for the game it is.

The skill of staying centered within self invites you to pull your attention back from the drama and respond to life instead of reacting. The distance of being centered within your being gives you space to navigate your experience through self-awareness.

In Case You Forgot.

You are love and light. You are goodness. You are compassion and sweetness. You are peace and joy and harmony. You are the teacher and the student. You are the healer and the healed. You are the comforter and the comforted. You are the giver and the receiver. You are serenity and bliss. You are all these things and more.

You get to choose whether you know it or not.

Right, Wrong, and Everything in Between.

Source's approval of you is unconditional and unwavering. He/She thinks you rock! Truly. Nothing you could do would disappoint Source. Because you and Source are the same thing. Source reflecting back to Source.

The most important question you can ask yourself is, "What kind of reflection do I want to be for Source?" When God looks at you, what does he see about himself/herself?

Don't beat yourself up about this reflection. No need. Do you really want to reflect guilt and fear back to God?

If you wish to change your reflection, change your state of being. It's truly that easy.

The Best Question Ever.

What do you want? It's the most important question you can continuously ask yourself. Desire is the electricity that keeps you alive!

The key is to choose consciously moment to moment. What do you want now? How about now? Life is one big on-going question made in small decisions throughout your life.

Make it easy on yourself. If you want to live differently, choose differently. There is no need to upend the apple cart of your life unless you like the drama. You can choose over and over what you value, how you want to feel, what's important, how you spend your time—bit by bit.

What the Heck am I Supposed to be Doing? Someone Tell Me!

"What's my purpose?" is a deeply rooted question for humans. This question plagues us because we are gifted with choices. We are blessed with the freedom to choose how we express who we are.

The confusion comes in when we believe that how we express is who we are. We then begin to doubt our preferences because we think we can make a wrong choice.

You are Source energy. You are God Stuff. You cannot make a bad choice because God created all options through you. Do you really believe God would give you choices that are not approved by him/her?

Every choice from God's perspective is fine. It's all good. Good because ultimately, you return to your true nature—your own version of God Stuff.

Ego.

Your ego is a blessing—a lens in which to see and experience Source. It's your unique personality that your Soul selected before you came into your body.

Your Soul is relishing being you and viewing life from this valuable perspective. This ego/personality aspect of you allows you to perceive yourself as separate from the whole, and to know what it feels like when you decide to join the whole again.

Sometimes if we believe we are only our ego/personality, we can clutter our perspective of life. This limited view is easily fixed when we remember our connection to the All-That-Is. It's also part of the awakening process.

God is the
inspiration
you feel.

Say What?

Believing you can't have something is the same thing as not wanting it. Your belief that it's not possible makes it impossible for you to experience it.

If you want something, believe that it's already here. Stop wanting. Start knowing that it's a done deal.

Shake Your Tail Feathers More.

Throw your hands in the air and dance to your own beat. Live. Rejoice. Be Who You Are. Let others be who they are. Try not to care what they think. Take chances. Live your life with abandon. Open. Receptive. Alive! That's how to be free within the glorious game of life.

What Do You NEED?

When you no longer need something to be a certain way, you find peace. When you no longer need a committed relationship, money in the bank, a skinny body, or a flashy boat in the harbor, you find yourself at your home address— Peace.

It's not that any of those lovely manifestations keep you from peace, but it's needing them to be there so that you have peace that pushes peace away.

So, want whatever you want and move towards that, but don't need anything to be just so in order to live in peace.

Corkscrew Kind of Life.

Progress. Let's get from point A to point B as fast as possible. Linear progression is such a human thing, and then on top of that, we make it into a competition. Sometimes even spiritually-minded folks want to be further along the path than others.

But life is richer and fuller than a straight line. Eternally you are more circular than linear. You circle into human life and out again. You dip back into Spirit and then re-emerge into physical. Finishing one phase only to start again at the beginning.

Imagine your eternal life as a giant corkscrew, circling and deepening at the same time. Your Soul enjoys getting into all the nooks and crannies of each experience to relish the deliciousness of it all.

What's the Big Deal About Self-Love?

Self-love is the key to fully expressing your true-self while in a human body. It's practically impossible to love God fully without loving his Creation—you. When you love you, you love God. It's all the same thing.

Your playful,
fun-loving nature
comes from God.

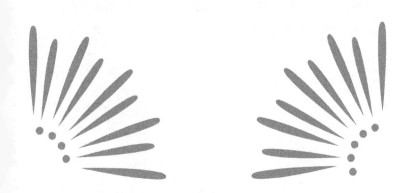

Joy is Your Default Setting.

A negative thought or belief has to work extremely hard to stay in your experience because your natural state is joy. That negative thought about yourself or something else really vies for your attention, saying, "Look at me, look at me!" It's like an unruly kid in a classroom who wants the teacher's attention. It will do just about anything to get noticed. But, just like a rowdy kid, if you ignore it and don't make a big fuss about it being there, it will naturally calm down and settle into the vibe of your whole joyful self.

All In.

The secret to genius or mastery is being all in. Believing it before seeing the results. Getting a glimpse of the creation completed and holding to that vision until it's manifested.

An easy way to do this is to find the feeling of the thing completed and become that vibrational state before the dream is realized.

Locus of Being.

Your essential self, your Soul-self, feels like you. It's your original Isness being expressed in you.

Sometimes, we believe when we allow our Soul to flow through us more fully, we will lose our personality. We'll become dull or boring. But, the exact opposite is true. You become even more of yourself. More alive, full, complete.

Nothing is ever lost or sacrificed. It all expands.

Magnificence.

Each Soul is glorious, amazing, beautiful, and magnificent.

No matter what the personality is choosing to do, be, or experience in this very human life, the Soul, the essence, is radiant. Each and every one of us.

Enlightenment and All That Jazz.

There is a lot of fuss about enlightenment. Don't worry, you'll get there eventually, and you've probably been there many times already. In a nutshell, enlightenment is the experience of knowing your core-self, your spirit-self, while in a body.

You know this immediately when you die and no longer have a body. Part of the fun of the human journey is knowing this while you're still in a form.

God knowing God. God reflecting God's perspective back to God. That's when it gets super fun!

Be true to you.

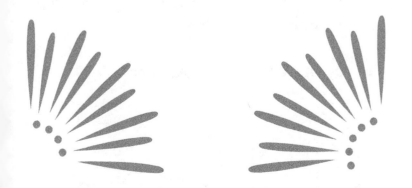

Make Peace with Your Desires.

Are you trying to talk yourself out of wanting something? Dissuading yourself is a difficult thing to do because your desire did not originate with you. It is an inspiration from your Soul—tiny desires and big ones. Follow them. Allow them. Make them okay. Act on them. Often they are not the end destination because that destination disappears once you get there, and another desire pops up.

The key is to be happy along the way as you hop from one desire to the next.

Happy and joyful in the meantime.

Easy-Peasy Joy.

Paying attention to what you like leads to a life of joy. Little by little, notice the things you like—the shiny, silver fish painting on the wall, the smell of honeysuckle on a summer's day, lightning bugs at dusk, baking cinnamon rolls.

The world is full of delights that are here to please you. When you choose to notice them, your life automatically becomes happier. Easy-peasy joy.

Are We All Headed in the Same Direction?

"Sort of" is the the most accurate answer. Let me break it down. We're all Source experiencing creation and creating through physicality. The goal is to be or remember our true-self—this beingness known as Source.

But, here is the kicker. Source is a lot of things. Source is multi-faceted. Love, light, appreciation, clarity, joy, enthusiasm, peace, serenity, calm, happiness, bliss, creative energy, and more! So your true-self may be expressed differently than my true-self.

That's why your uniqueness is incredibly valuable to the whole!

The Perfect Trifecta.

Body, Mind, and Soul. You've got everything you need. All the tools that are required.

The Soul-self plants a desire. The mind-self chooses to listen to the desire or not—the body-self acts out the mind's choice.

If the body and mind choose to agree with the Soul's desire, the Soul gets to experience itself. It gets to know what it's like to be a Soul in a human body. It gets to feel its Soul-self. Glorious creation!

One In the Same.

Because you come from God, from the Source where everything originates, you have this deep desire within your being to reconnect with God in your human life. This pull to God strikes at different times and in different ways for each of us. For some, loss or grief ignites our hunger. For others, it's the creative urge to make that hones our inner listening. Some seek comfort or peace or serenity. Whatever calls you home to Spirit is the perfect thing that you'll listen to at that moment in your life.

If you look back over your life you will notice that Spirit has called you in many ways. Never giving up on you.

Everything
is Energy.

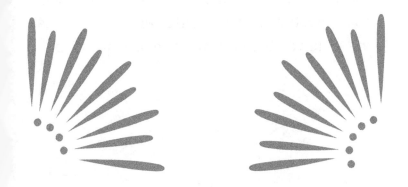

Let Them Believe Whatever They Want.

Your Soul's wish for you is to to harmonize with your Soul-self. Your Soul calls you to Soul-alignment by using what excites you and lights you up on the inside.

Sometimes, to follow this call, you have to ignore other people's opinions so you can hear your Soul's wisdom. This is so important—it does not matter what anyone else thinks of you. It only matters how you feel about yourself. If you hold steady to the frequency of who you really are, then it won't matter what anyone else thinks of you because you'll be Soul satisfied.

Where Do You Live?

Many of us believe that our Soul lives within our body because we feel it in the body when we are moved by Spirit. But your Soul is way more immense than anything a human body could contain.

In reality, your body is housed within your Soul.

Your Soul is this beautiful, magnificent energy surrounding and permeating your body. Not only does it encompasses your body, but it extends outward, mixing with the Unified Field of Possibilities in which everything arises. It touches the All That Is.

Understanding this is part of the remembering.

Good Enough.

Self-acceptance is the quickest path to being in harmony with your Soul's desire to experience self-love.

Accept everything.

Embrace it all.

Judge none of it.

Love the whole kit and caboodle.

Make all parts of yourself okay.

Let it all be there.

Surrender to Your Dreams.

What if your grandest dream for yourself is the same thing as God's will for you?

God wants what you want for you.

At the core of your being, you are the same energy as God. God would never deny God. What's the point in that?

God is bliss, happiness, love, light, fun, and joy. He/she will give you anything you want that you believe will evoke these emotions.

Give in to your dreams. They are God-inspired.

Transformation.

Transformation is the willingness to show up where you are—differently.

Surrender
all Resistance.

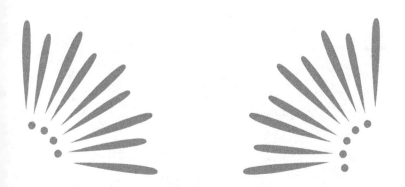

God Doesn't Forgive.

God doesn't need to forgive because Source never perceives us as wrong. Source sees us as whole, perfect, and divine. Source is never judging us or withdrawing its appreciation of us.

Unconditional Love at its grandest!

The Sky is the Limit—Or Maybe Not?

You are an unlimited being. You are a powerful creator. Your only limits are self-imposed.

You unleash your potential by letting go of your limitations. Just like a hot air balloon rises when its weights are thrown off, so too do you soar when you let go of your unneeded baggage.

Personal Power.

Assume your power by knowing with your whole being that you are responsible for creating your life.

Don't blame anyone else—parents, government, society, or biology. When you blame someone else, you give away your power.

You are a creator who creates your own perception, and perception is reality. Own your power.

Lighten Up Already.

Try not to take life too seriously. (Enlightenment is all about lightening up.)

Face life with a twinkle in your eye and a smile in your heart. Let life surprise and delight you. Enjoy it my friends!

Neutral.

All events are neutral. Nothing is really good or bad. It's our personal perception that makes it feel positive or negative. When you realize this, it takes the sting out of life. You begin to trust the unfolding of things. You begin to trust the process by not resisting the process.

So look out onto the world and bless it. If the world brings up the stuff that closes you off from your heart, from your loving nature, bless that too.

Let all the junk rise to the surface and see it calmly with neutral eyes as things that once served you but no longer work because you've grown, changed, and transformed.

Trust the Cosmos.

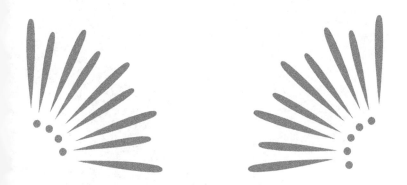

Fun to Ponder.

Your Soul does not need a body. It can be a Soul without the body. But, the body needs a Soul. It can't live without the presence of Spirit.

Your Dreams Are Real.

Your wildest dreams have already come true! They exist within the field of possibilities. They are REAL.

For your dreams to manifest into the physical world, they need your permission. You grant them physical life through your attention, frequency, and beliefs.

To manifest your dreams, start at the end. Feel for the dream. Match its frequency and its intensity. Believe that it exists. Trust that it is happening. The feeling of it complete is what you're reaching for. Because it is already done.

Soul-Based Reality.

Becoming your Soul isn't about losing yourself. It's about becoming more of who you truly are. So, you don't give up your freedom, laughter, humor, sassiness, or friskiness. You become more of those things not to please others, but to please yourself.

What Lights Your Fire?

If you are looking for your purpose, wanting to know who you truly are, what you really came to be, then follow your passion. Follow your excitement. Those feelings come from your Soul-self. When you feel excited about something, you are in the same frequency as your Soul-self on the subject.

Excitement, passion, enthusiasm, and eagerness are indicators that you're being true to yourself.

You Exist.

Your existence is pretty obvious. You're here in a body aware of yourself. But, did you know that your sheer presence is what makes you valuable?

You exist. That makes you part of the whole. The whole could not be whole without you.

Because you exist, you will never not exist. This means you are worthy of existence and will always be valuable no matter what you choose to do.

Follow the fun.

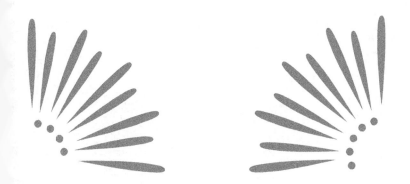

Dreams, Desires, Inspiration.

Desires are states of consciousness that want embodiment. They want to be experienced by you. They want to live through you.

As you change what you believe about yourself, you'll automatically adjust your desires. They will morph and grow with you.

Accept. Accept. Accept.

It can't be said enough times—acceptance of what is leads to a peaceful heart. When you look at something you don't like, whether, in yourself or the world, the first step to changing it is accepting it.

It sounds backward to accept something you don't want, but resisting the thing makes it stronger in your experience. When you make something okay, it magically releases its hold on you.

You Are a Giant Communication Device.

You are a giant, walking communication device. You are continually receiving input from your outer-world and your inner-world.

You are also sending out a vibrations of what you want to experience. You set the tone of what you receive by emitting a vibe or attitude.

God Isn't Keeping Score.

You're not here to prove anything. Not one thing. God isn't keeping score so why are you? Nothing you do will make you worthy. Nothing you accomplish makes you more valuable.

You are WORTHY. Period.

So, go out and have fun. Mix it up. Enjoy your life with all of your being because God is already enjoying your life through you.

Your Wish is the Universe's Command.

The Universe is responding to your requests with a YES every time. The Universe desires to fulfill your demands because it wishes for you to be joyful. Your joy gives the Universe joy. Your happiness, your satisfaction, your appreciation, and your love delights the Universe. It would never choose to say no to this beautiful process of creation and appreciation.

A Party Going on Here!

It's a fantastic time to be alive! The attention of the entire Universe is focused on us right now. We are experiencing an incredible transformation and every energy being of good-will is concentrating on our reality.

From the broader-perspective, beings across the Universe are cheering for us, supporting us, loving us, sending us well-wishes, and offering their wisdom. This is a galactic party honoring humans.

Inner Ear.

You are a very wise, ancient being. At your core, you are the same as your creator. You contain the Universe within you. So, when you lose touch with this knowingness, begin to listen for it with your inner ear. This inner ear listens for the whisper of the Soul. This inner ear is trained to hear your personal truth and knows it when it feels it.

Reach for relaxed happiness.

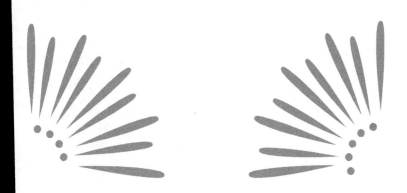

Comfort Zone.

Comfort. Security. Stability. We tend to gravitate towards those feeling because we feel safe when there, but life is about expansion. Your joy is not based on staying still. Your Soul wants to change, move, and grow. No need to push your evolution, but you don't want to stifle it either.

When you're ready, allow yourself to leap into the unknown future. It's the exhilaration of the ride that really gets your juices flowing!

The Secret to Life is to Feel Good.

Deep within you, you know that you're supposed to be up to something important while you're here on earth. That important thing is feeling good. Connecting to your inner-joy.

In your joy, you are valuable to the Universe, you are clear, you are receptive, and you are flowing Source-energy every where you go.

Isn't it fabulous that this Universe is set up that you are most beneficial when you feel great?

Life is But a Dream.

Part of waking up is knowing that you walk in a dream world. Part of the fun is being aware of the dream and unaffected by the dream at the same time. The dream is temporary. It is ever-changing. Most importantly, it is responding to your focus, thoughts, and attitude.

Don't Be So Stingy.

God is your Source, and your Source flows through you. You come from the same place where time originates, where abundance comes from, where love lives, where happiness dwells, where bliss is born. So, stop being stingy with yourself. Don't limit the power available to you. Unleash it!

Inside-Out.

Change occurs from the inside out. Change is about shifting your perspective, choosing what you give your attention to, where you put your focus.

If you want to change the world, you start by transforming how you see the world. Change your personal view of the outside world by altering how you feel in your inner-world. You can't change the reflection in the mirror by adjusting the mirror.

You are free
to choose.

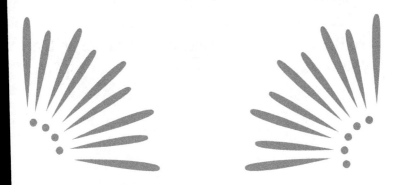

Growth Spurt.

As a people, humans are experiencing a growth spurt—a time of sped up evolution. It is unprecedented. Never before on such a massive scale have we realized this beautiful blending of our human-self and our Soul-self.

This blending has been occurring in humans for some time in a sort of spotty fashion—Jesus, Buddha, Gandhi, Mother Teresa, and others throughout history. But now the blending is happening in oodles of us.

You're here for the acceleration. You are on the fast track, my friend!

Role Play.

Souls choose the human experience for reasons that humans don't always understand. We pick life situations from that broader perspective that can be so hard to wrap the human mind around. But, the Soul sees physical life as a game; a temporary adventure. So it's not too concerned about comfort or status.

So, try not to judge someone else's life experience. You don't know what they signed up for.

Lover of Life.

The greatest joy is to love life. Be the lover of life because when you love, you experience love. Loving is being in harmony with your Soul.

Loving is not your duty. It's a pleasure. A gift to yourself first, and then to others because you receive the delicious benefit of feeling the love first. It's a direct experience.

The bonus is when you emit love, the world will then reflect back to you the love you have given so freely.

God's Grace.

God's grace is available and abundant. This goodness is free to anyone. The only requirement is that you accept it.

God is All of It.

In Gratitude

Scotty My love, thank you for your never-ending support encouraging me to be true to myself. I'm blessed you are my husband and my best friend. Forever, and ever, my love.

Winna Thank you for being a shining example of the most generous spirit I know. I love you, Momma.

All my teachers along my path I am humbled by the love and support I've been shown.

My Vibe Tribe Thank you for your unwavering love.

Source, God, The-All-That-Is, Universe, The Cosmos What a gift my life is! Thank you!

About the Author

Michele makes her home in Memphis, Tennessee, with husband Scott and chocolate Labrador, Dewey. The Little Book of Big Knowing is Michele's first book, but probably not her last. You can discover more about Michele's work on her website: www.michelesammons.com.

CPSIA information can be obtained
at www.ICGtesting.com
Printed in the USA
LVHW082131280521
688849LV00003B/323

9 781736 168608